PIANO • VOCAL • GUITAR

Forrest Gump
The Soundtrack

ISBN 0-7935-3786-X

HAL•LEONARD™
CORPORATION

7777 W. BLUEMOUND RD. P.O. BOX 13819 MILWAUKEE, WI 53213

Forrest Gump
The Soundtrack

HOUND DOG

Words and Music by JERRY LEIBER
and MIKE STOLLER

Medium Rock

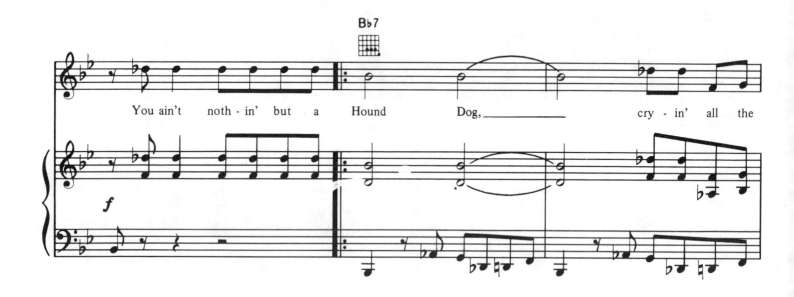

You ain't noth-in' but a Hound Dog,_____ cry-in' all the

time. You ain't noth-in' but a Hound Dog,_____

REBEL 'ROUSER

By DUANE EDDY
and LEE HAZLEWOOD

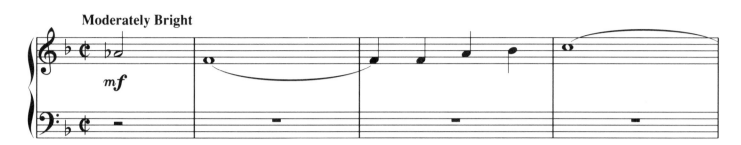

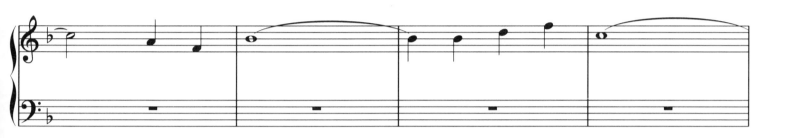

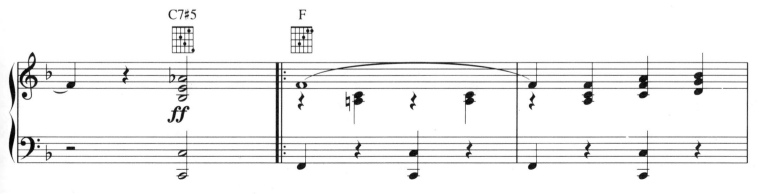

WALK RIGHT IN

Words and Music by GUS CANNON
and H. WOODS

LAND OF A THOUSAND DANCES

Words and Music by
CHRIS KENNER

BLOWIN' IN THE WIND

Words and Music by
BOB DYLAN

FORTUNATE SON

Words and Music by
JOHN FOGERTY

BUT I DO
(a/k/a I DON'T KNOW WHY)

Words and Music by ROBERT C. GUIDRY
and PAUL GAYTEN

I don't know why I love you but I do.
can't sleep nights be - cause I feel so rest - less,

don't know why I cry so, but I do.
don't know what to do, I feel so help - less.

on - ly know I'm lone - ly and that I want you on - ly,
since you've been a - way. I cry both night and day,

I CAN'T HELP MYSELF
(SUGAR PIE, HONEY BUNCH)

Words and Music by BRIAN HOLLAND,
LAMONT DOZIER and EDWARD HOLLAND

RESPECT

Words and Music by
OTIS REDDING

32

my pro-per res-pect when you get home. Yeah,
is give me some here when you get home. Yeah,

ba – by, when you get home.
ba – by, when you get home.

R – E – S – P – E – C – T, find out what it means to me, R – E – S – P – E – C – T,

Repeat and fade out

take out T – C – P, a lit-tle re – pect.

RAINY DAY WOMEN #12 & 35

Words and Music by
BOB DYLAN

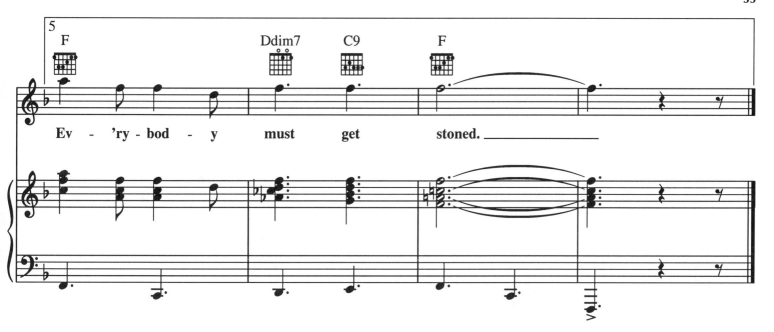

5
F   Ddim7   C9   F

Ev - 'ry - bod - y   must   get   stoned. _____

Additional Lyrics

2. Well, they'll stone ya when you're walkin' 'long the street.
   They'll stone ya when you're tryin' to keep your seat.
   They'll stone ya when you're walkin' on the floor.
   They'll stone ya when you're walkin' to the door.
   But I would not feel so all alone,
   Everybody must get stoned.

3. They'll stone ya when you're at the breakfast table.
   They'll stone ya when you are young and able.
   They'll stone ya when you're tryin' to make a buck.
   They'll stone ya and then they'll say, "Good luck."
   Tell ya what, I would not feel so all alone,
   Everybody must get stoned.

4. Well, they'll stone you and say that it's the end.
   Then they'll stone you and then they'll come back again.
   They'll stone you when you're riding in your car.
   They'll stone you when you're playing your guitar.
   Yes, but I would not feel so all alone,
   Everybody must get stoned.

5. Well, they'll stone you when you walk all alone.
   They'll stone you when you are walking home.
   They'll stone you and then say you are brave.
   They'll stone you when you are set down in your grave.
   But I would not feel so all alone,
   Everybody must get stoned.

SLOOP JOHN B

Words and Music by
BRIAN WILSON

CALIFORNIA DREAMIN'

Words and Music by JOHN PHILLIPS
and MICHELLE PHILLIPS

Medium Rock beat

All the leaves are brown, And the sky___ is grey.___

I've been___ for a walk on a win-ter's day.___

I'd be safe and warm,___ if I was in L. A.___
If I did-n't tell her___ I could leave___ to-day.___

40

FOR WHAT IT'S WORTH

Words and Music by
STEPHEN STILLS

WHAT THE WORLD NEEDS NOW IS LOVE

Lyric by HAL DAVID
Music by BURT BACHARACH

With a jazz waltz feel

mf

What the world needs now is love, sweet love, It's the on-ly thing ____ that there's just ____ too

BREAK ON THROUGH
(TO THE OTHER SIDE)

Words and Music by
THE DOORS

Additional lyrics

3. I found an island in your arms, a country in your eyes,
   Arms that chain, eyes that lie.
   To Chorus:

4. Made the scene from week to week, day to day, hour to hour,
   The gate is straight, deep and wide.
   To Chorus:

MRS. ROBINSON

Words and Music by
PAUL SIMON

VOLUNTEERS

Words and Music by PAUL KANTNER
and MARTY BALIN

Moderate Rock

Look what's hap-p'ning on __ the streets.   Got to rev-o-lu-tion, got __ to rev-o-lu-tion.

vol - un - teers __ of A-mer - i - ca, __

vol - un - teers __ of A-mer - i - ca, __

vol - un - teers __ of A-mer - i - ca, __

vol - un - teers __ of A-mer - i - ca. __

Instrumental ad lib.

LET'S GET TOGETHER

Words and Music by
CHET POWERS

1. Love is but the song we sing, and fear's the way we
2. Some will come and some will go, and we shall sure - ly
3. If you heard the song I sing, you must un - der-

AQUARIUS/LET THE SUNSHINE IN

Words by JAMES RADO and GEROME RAGNI
Music by GALT MacDERMOT

SAN FRANCISCO
(BE SURE TO WEAR SOME FLOWERS IN YOUR HAIR)

Words and Music by
JOHN PHILLIPS

TURN! TURN! TURN!
(TO EVERYTHING THERE IS A SEASON)

Words from the Book of Ecclesiastes
Adaptation and Music by PETE SEEGER

EVERYBODY'S TALKIN'
(ECHOES)

Words and Music by
FRED NEIL

84

JOY TO THE WORLD

Words and Music by
HOYT AXTON

STONED LOVE

Words and Music by FRANK E. WILSON
and YENNIK SAMOHT

RAINDROPS KEEP FALLIN'
ON MY HEAD

Lyric by HAL DAVID
Music by BURT BACHARACH

head. They keep fall-in' so I just did me some talk-in' to the

sun. And I said I did-n't like the way he got things

done. Sleep-in' on the job. Those rain - drops are fall-in' on my

head. They keep fall-in'! But there's one thing I know

soon be turn - in' red. Cry - in's not for me 'cause

I'm nev - er gon - na stop the rain by com-plain-in'. Be - cause I'm

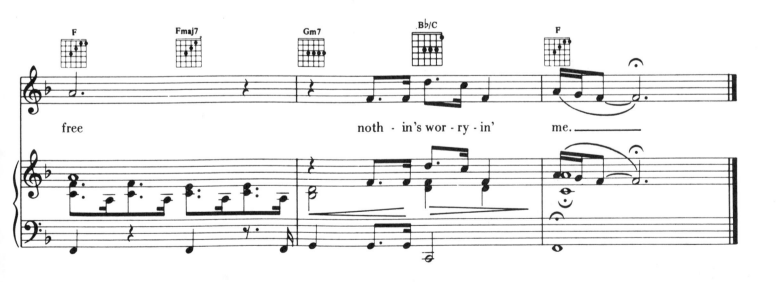

free noth - in's wor - ry - in' me.

MR. PRESIDENT
(HAVE PITY ON THE WORKING MAN)

Words and Music by
RANDY NEWMAN

We've tak - en all you've giv - en.
We ain't ask - ing you to love us.

It's ___ get - ting hard to make ___ a liv - ing.
You ___ may place your - self high ___ a - bove us.

Mis - ter Pres - i - dent, have pit - y on ___ the work - ing
Mis - ter Pres - i - dent, have pit - y on ___ the work - ing

SWEET HOME ALABAMA

Words and Music by RONNIE VAN ZANT,
ED KING and GARY ROSSINGTON

I miss 'ole' 'bam - y once a - gain___ *(And I think it's a sin.)*

Verse

2. Well, I heard Mis - ter Young   sing a -

bout her.   Well, I heard ole Neil___ put her

down.   Well, I hope Neil Young   will re -

102

ADDITIONAL LYRICS

Verse 4.   Now Muscle Shoals has got the Swampers
           And they've been known to pick a tune or two
           Lord they get me off so much
           They pick me up when I'm feeling blue
           Now how about you.

Repeat Chorus and Fade

IT KEEPS YOU RUNNIN'

Words and Music by
MICHAEL McDONALD

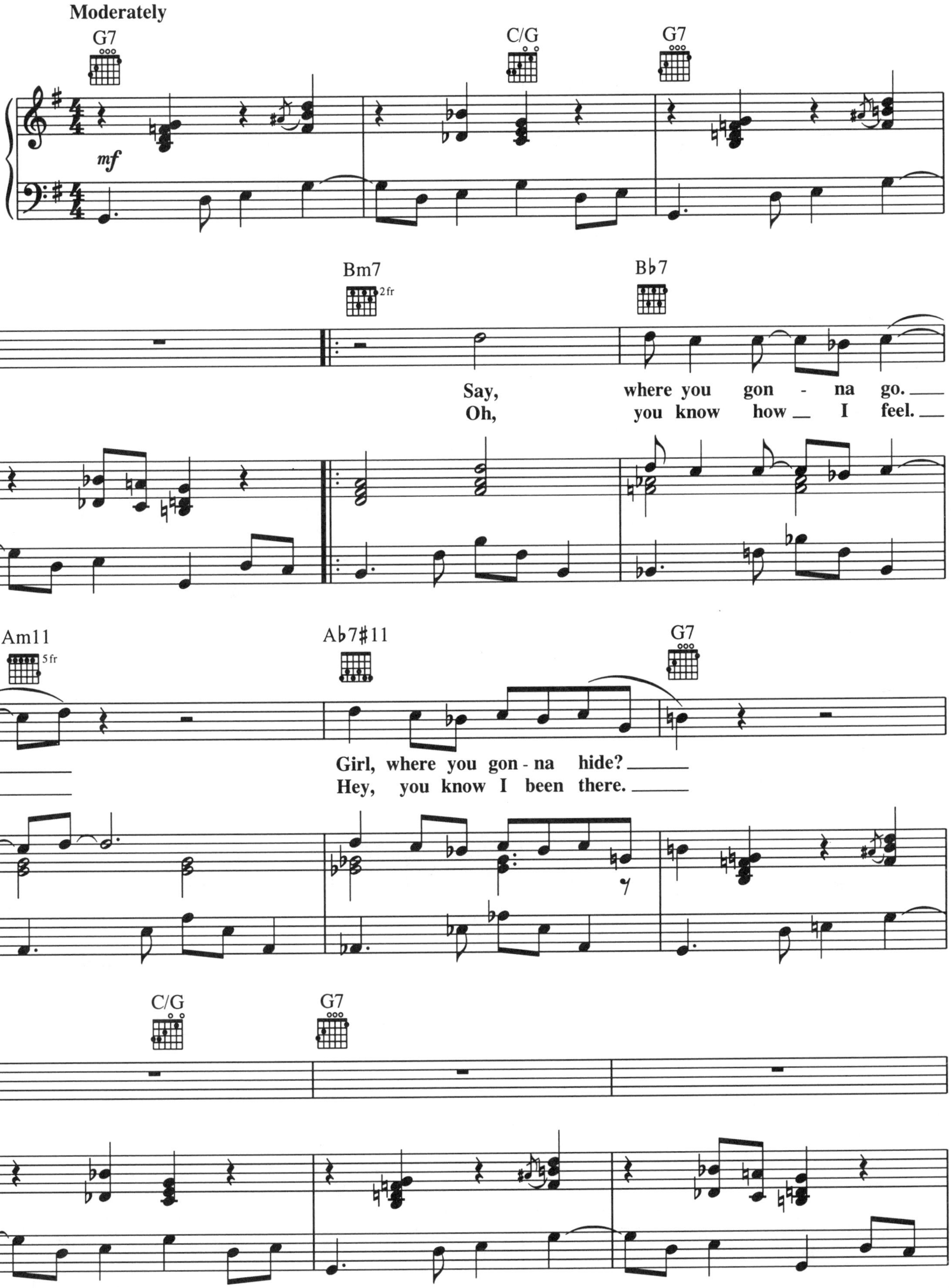

Moderately
G7
C/G
G7
mf
Bm7
Bb7
Say, where you gon - na go.
Oh, you know how I feel.
Am11
Ab7#11
G7
Girl, where you gon - na hide?
Hey, you know I been there.
C/G
G7

I'VE GOT TO USE MY IMAGINATION

Words and Music by GERRY GOFFIN
and BARRY GOLDBERG

AGAINST THE WIND

Words and Music by
BOB SEGER

ON THE ROAD AGAIN

Words and Music by
WILLIE NELSON

Verse 2:
On the road again.
Goin' places that I've never been.
Seein' things that I may never see again,
And I can't wait to get on the road again.
(To 2nd ending)

FORREST GUMP SUITE

Music by ALAN SILVESTRI

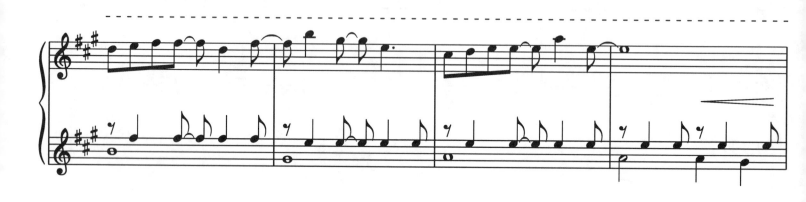

Passionately